DATE DUE

JUN 0 8 2011

SOFT
HOUSE

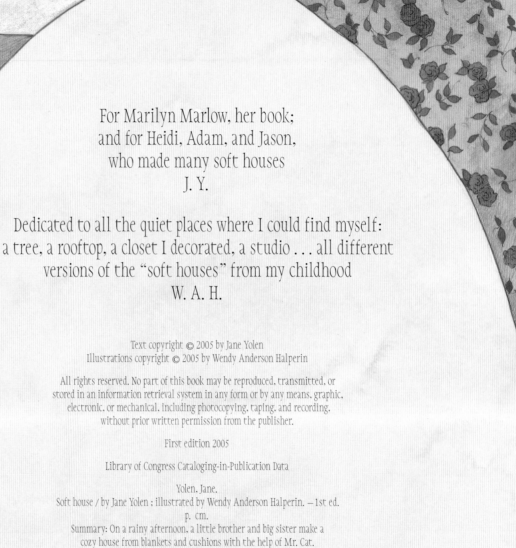

For Marilyn Marlow, her book;
and for Heidi, Adam, and Jason,
who made many soft houses
J. Y.

Dedicated to all the quiet places where I could find myself:
a tree, a rooftop, a closet I decorated, a studio . . . all different
versions of the "soft houses" from my childhood
W. A. H.

Text copyright © 2005 by Jane Yolen
Illustrations copyright © 2005 by Wendy Anderson Halperin

First edition 2005

Library of Congress Cataloging-in-Publication Data

Yolen, Jane.
Soft house / by Jane Yolen ; illustrated by Wendy Anderson Halperin. — 1st ed.
p. cm.
Summary: On a rainy afternoon, a little brother and big sister make a
cozy house from blankets and cushions with the help of Mr. Cat.
ISBN 0-7636-1697-4
[1. Play — Fiction. 2. Brothers and sisters — Fiction. 3. Cats — Fiction.]
I. Halperin, Wendy Anderson, ill. II. Title.
PZ7.Y78So 2005
[E] — dc22   2004051898

2 4 6 8 10 9 7 5 3 1

Printed in China

This book was typeset in Integrity.
The illustrations were done in pencil and watercolor.

Candlewick Press
2067 Massachusetts Avenue
Cambridge, Massachusetts 02140

visit us at www.candlewick.com

SOFT
HOUSE

Jane Yolen

illustrated by
Wendy Anderson Halperin

CANDLEWICK PRESS
CAMBRIDGE, MASSACHUSETTS

It's raining.
I watch the drops slide down the window,
leaving trails for my fingers to follow.
Davey makes a face. Mama says someday his face
is going to freeze that way. I'd like to see that.
"I hate rain," says Davey. "There's nothing to do."

"We could play checkers," I say.
"You always win."
"We could play school."
"You're always the teacher." He
makes another face, then lies face
down on the big sofa and cries.

"I could read you a book."
Davey looks up. There are no
tears on his face. "It's my turn
to read."

"You can't read."

"I can read pictures."

This time I make the face. "Pictures
don't count." Then, feeling mean,
I add, "You can't count, either."
"Can."
"Can't."
"Can!"
He throws himself back down on
the sofa and wails. LOUD.

Mama calls from the kitchen. "Alison Isabelle, what are you doing to your little brother?"

"NOTHING!" I shout, then turn to Davey. "Yet."

He smiles. What a big faker. Dad calls those his crocodile tears.

"I know," says Davey. "Let's play Soft House." It's his favorite game.

I like playing Soft House, too.
I was the one who made it up. I like
everything except for the upstairs
part—the long, dark, windowless
hall. I don't like to go up alone.

"Only if you get the blankets,"
I tell Davey.

He frowns. "But it's scary up there."

I think hard. There must be some way to convince him. Then I have it. "Take Mr. Cat. He can step on the shadows and catch them with his claws."

"Where is Mr. Cat?" asks Davey,
already feeling braver.
"He was here a minute ago,"
I tell him.

Quickly we search the room
and find Mr. Cat curled up on the
wood stack, probably dreaming
about the sun.

Davey picks him up. Mr. Cat stretches
and complains. But when Davey puts
him on the stairs, Mr. Cat is eager to
go up. Davey runs after him.

At first I'm happy Davey has gone upstairs. But he takes a long time. Much too long for just a few blankets.

I go to the foot of the stairs and call his name. "Davey?" Then louder. "DAVEY!" It's no good. I have to go find him.

And suddenly there's Davey, with a mountain of blankets. Mr. Cat is right behind him, fishing for wool fish with silent claws.

"What took you so long?" I ask.

"Mr. Cat was slow," he said. "And he sat on the blankets."

"You're very brave," I say.

"I know," Davey tells me. "Besides, Mama says you can't be scared when you have a friend to take care of. Like Mr. Cat."

I nod. *Or a little brother,* I think.

I take the blankets from Davey.
The big yellow one from Mama's
bed. The blue one from Davey's.
The green one from my own bed.
And my silky blanket, Macarina,
who lives under my pillow.

I dump them all on the sofa.
Davey jumps into the blankets.
Mr. Cat sits on his lap.
"Soft House," I say. It's my job
to make it.

I take the cushions off the sofa
and the big snuggle chair and balance
them against the sofa for walls.
Pillows make the roof. They all fall
over, and I try again.

Davey laughs. "I'll help," he says.

Usually I don't let him—but he
did go up the stairs by himself.

"Okay," I say. It's a kind of apology.
Davey shoves Mr. Cat from his lap
and gets up.

On our third try, everything works.
Walls . . . roof . . . and an opening
wide enough for a door. We spread
the blankets over the top.

Davey crawls inside.
"Did you remember the flashlight?"
he calls out, his voice muffled.
"Of course." I roll the flashlight in.
"And the cookies?"

Mama comes in with a plate of peanut-butter-crunch-and-chocolate-chip cookies. The best.

I push the plate through the Soft House door. Then I take Macarina and crawl in.

It's dark inside, but not a
scary dark. Upstairs is scary
because it's a long dark. This
is a round dark.

Besides, Davey is here, and you can't be scared when you have a little brother to take care of.

Inside Soft House, the little
warm flashlight sun makes lovely
round shadows.

The shadows dance all over the
inside of Soft House while Davey and
I eat the peanut-butter-crunch-and-
chocolate-chip cookies.

Mr. Cat closes his eyes
and purrs.